THE Motherhood CLUB
Making a Difference One Mom at a Time
mc

The Busy Mom's Guide to Wisdom

Wisdom

A GUIDED JOURNAL

Lisa Whelchel

HOWARD
PUBLISHING CO

OUR PURPOSE AT HOWARD PUBLISHING IS TO:

- *Increase* faith in the hearts of growing Christians
- *Inspire* holiness in the lives of believers
- *Instill* hope in the hearts of struggling people everywhere

BECAUSE HE'S COMING AGAIN!

The Busy Mom's Guide to Wisdom © 2006 by Lisa Whelchel
All rights reserved. Printed in the United States of America
Published by Howard Publishing Co., Inc.
3117 North Seventh Street, West Monroe, LA 71291-2227
www.howardpublishing.com

06   07   08   09   10   11   12   13   14   15   10 9 8 7 6 5 4 3 2

Edited by Between the Lines
Cover design by Diane Whisner
Cover illustrations by Cindy Sartain
Interior design by John Mark Luke Designs
Interior illustrations by John Mark Luke
Paraphrased scriptures by Lisa Whelchel

ISBN 1-58229-488-7

This book of wisdom is dedicated

to my friend and manager,

Ron Smith, *a real wise guy!*

His humor, loyalty, hard work,

and wisdom are daily gifts to me.

As iron sharpens iron, a friend sharpens a friend.

PROVERBS 27:17 NLT

Contents

Contents

The Busy Mom's Guide to Wisdom

How many times have you thrown up your hands in frustration and cried, "I just don't know what to do"? When our children are babies, we're bewildered as to how to console them. During the toddler years, we can't figure out how to keep up with them. As our little ones grow older, we have education questions, friendship dilemmas, and safety issues.

I don't even want to *talk* about the teenage years and the sense of utter helplessness that often accompanies them. The questions never end. Even after our kids' hormones settle down a bit, we still have matters such as college, marriage, and careers to worry about. I don't think mothers ever stop worrying.

We worry because we know deep inside, somewhere down there where the motherly instinct resides, that our children's lives are really out of our hands. We can't hold them tightly enough, we can't control their environment adequately, we can't protect them sufficiently, and we can't lecture them as long as

Introduction

necessary. When it comes right down to it, even giving our all to ensure a healthy, happy future just isn't enough.

We recognize our limitations; we know we need help. So we spend hours on the phone with our friends seeking advice. We spend hundreds of dollars on the latest books promising the keys to success. We spend untold amounts of energy running around looking for help because we know that the answers we're seeking are beyond ourselves. And, intuitively, we know they're even beyond this world.

Sincere moms everywhere are looking to astrology, angel guides, enlightenment, the cosmos, meditation, and many more paths that promise to lead them to ultimate wisdom. They're doing exactly what Wisdom instructs them to do. Wisdom says, "Those who seek me diligently will find me" (Proverbs 8:17 NKJV). But tragically, these moms are looking in the wrong places, so they aren't finding the answers they so desperately need.

Then where in the world do we begin? There's a clue—God created the world, and He created us. So He's going to be the One who knows the answers to how to make our lives and the lives of our children work. God has the wisdom for which we've been searching. All we have to do is listen.

Now if Wisdom could talk, what would it say? No need to guess—there's actually a recorded conversation:

I, wisdom, was with the LORD when he began his work, long before he made anything else. I was created in the very beginning, even before the world began. I was born before there were oceans, or springs overflowing with water, before the hills were there, before the mountains were put in place. God had not made the earth or fields, not even the first dust of the earth. I was there when God put the skies in place, when he stretched the horizon over the oceans, when he made the clouds above and put the deep underground springs in place. I was there when he ordered the sea not to go beyond the borders he had set. I was there when he laid the earth's foundation. I was like a child by his side. I was delighted every day, enjoying his presence all the time, enjoying the whole world, and delighted with all its people.

Now, my children, listen to me, because those who follow my ways are happy. (PROVERBS 8:22–32 NCV)

It appears that going back to the beginning for our answers was even smarter than we thought. Not only is God, our Creator, there, but so is Wisdom! We've found what we've been looking for. What else does Wisdom have to say? A lot!

The book of Proverbs is so chock-full of Wisdom that it's often referred to as the Book of Wisdom. Proverbs has been my favorite portion of Scripture since I was a little girl. I think the reason I love it is because it's practical. One of my favorite

Introduction

definitions of *wisdom* is "supernatural truth lived out in a practical way." That's exactly what the book of Proverbs shows us.

Another reason I'm drawn to this book is because it's written specifically for children, regardless of age. In the very first chapter it says, "Hear, my son, your father's instruction, and forsake not your mother's teaching" (Proverbs 1:8). When I was a little girl, I understood that these practical words of wisdom were not only written from a parent to a child, but even more personally, they were written to me, a child of God, from my heavenly Father. Now that I have children of my own, I enjoy the added blessing of teaching my kids the practical lessons I've learned from my Father.

I wrote *The Busy Mom's Guide to Wisdom* to bring the ageless wisdom of the book of Proverbs into the lives of today's moms.

There's a temptation to think that the Bible is a sacred but irrelevant book written for a generation long past. Too many *thees* and *thous* and prophets and genealogies to offer any application for our lives today. I'll let the Bible itself respond to that accusation: "What has been is what will be, and what has been done is what will be done, and there is nothing new under the sun" (Ecclesiastes 1:9).

We are tackling the same challenges the mothers in the Bible had to deal with thousands of years ago. The Word of God has quite a bit to say about discipline, obedience, marriages, finances, anger, fear, and everything else we face. As you'll see, moms back then asked most of the same questions we do today. And the answer is still the same: "Jesus Christ is the same yesterday and today and forever" (Hebrews 13:8).

How to Use This Book

The Busy Mom's Guide to Wisdom contains fifty-two entries. With that in mind, you may want to read one entry per week, meditating on it for those seven days, while asking God to help you apply His timeless wisdom to your everyday circumstances. Or you may choose to read one a day, asking the Lord to search your heart and mold you into His image as you submit to the truth of His Word.

In true busy-mom fashion, I can also understand if you simply keep this book by your nightstand. Then, whenever you have just enough energy at the end of the day, you can pick it up and trust the sovereignty of the Lord to confirm something He's already been speaking to you about in your spirit.

However you choose to take advantage of the wisdom within these pages, I have full confidence that you won't be the same when you turn the last page. Sound cocky? Nah. I'm just repeating what God Himself says about His Word: "The same thing is true of the words I speak. They will not return

Introduction

to me empty. They make the things happen that I want to happen, and they succeed in doing what I send them to do" (Isaiah 55:11 NCV).

Each entry is based directly on God's Word and focuses on an issue I have faced as a woman and a mom, and I assume you have too. Let's look at the five elements of each entry.

Wisdom for Today

For every topic, I've chosen a verse from the book of Proverbs. The first thing I do is paraphrase it, or put it into my own words. I sincerely hope you're not offended by my doing this. I am in no way, shape, or form trying to rewrite the Holy Scriptures. That's not my intention at all.

I've just found that when I look at a scripture and think about how it might sound if it were written in my time and in my vernacular, it helps me apply the timeless wisdom of God to my life today.

Wisdom for Living

The next element is in response to the question, *How can I practically live out this truth that I've learned from God's Word?* I've simply jotted down my own thoughts in relation to the passage in hopes that you might find some application from my personal insights.

Wisdom to Pray

For me, the quickest way to be changed by the revelation in God's Word is to immediately pause and pray. I have every intention of making any adjustments the Holy Spirit reveals to me through the Scriptures, but I've failed in my own strength enough times to know that the real power to succeed comes only from the Lord. Thankfully, He tells us that all we have to do is ask and believe that He answers: "Whatever you ask in prayer, you will receive, if you have faith" (Matthew 21:22).

Now it's your turn to ask. After my prayer I've included some lines where you can write your own personal prayer asking God to help you apply the wisdom in His Word to your life and circumstances. What a wonderful record this will be of the privilege we have of serving a God who hears and answers our prayers. Don't forget to go back and jot a quick note of thanksgiving and praise. Then share the story of God's faithfulness with your children and watch their faith grow!

Wisdom in Action

God definitely works most powerfully from the inside out in answer to our prayers. But that doesn't mean we should just sit back and do nothing. When God speaks to us, there's always a necessary point of action, in addition to believing, that we need to take. The Bible says, when talking about a man who believed

Introduction

God, "He was trusting God so much that he was willing to do whatever God told him to do. His faith was made complete by what he did—by his actions" (James 2:22 NLT).

For each session, I've supplied you with some blank lines to write out a commitment that stems from what you learned from the proverb we've been sharing. Think about how God's wisdom applies to your life—to the things you do every day, to the way you interact with the people in your life, and to how you handle your many responsibilities. You'll notice that each line begins with, "Today I will . . ." I want you to think in concrete terms about something you can begin to put into practice on the very day you write it. That doesn't mean you'll bring the change to completion in one day, but what you write should be a practical step that you can begin to implement right away.

For example, when you read Proverbs 3:5, "Trust in the LORD with all your heart and lean not on your own understanding" (NIV), you could write, "Today I will stop trying to figure out how to fix my own problems. Instead of allowing worry to dominate my thoughts, I will choose to praise God for His power and faithfulness and trust that He will intervene on my behalf."

Wisdom from God

I've saved the best for last—the pure Word of God, untainted by my personal paraphrase, point of view, or prayer, appears at the end of each entry. May I recommend that you write each proverb on a piece of paper, sticky note, or index card and refer to it throughout the week or day? You won't even have to make a conscious effort to memorize the scripture. By simply repeating the verse over and over again, saying it aloud as much as possible for additional power, you'll suddenly discover that you've successfully hidden God's Word in your heart. Psalm 119:11 says, "I have hidden your word in my heart that I might not sin against you" (NIV).

Wow! Are you as excited as I am about the change God is going to bring about in our hearts and lives and, subsequently, our families? By simply applying His timeless wisdom to our practical needs, we can see heaven meet earth, *super* join *natural*, and the Word come to life.

> If you need wisdom—if you want to know what God wants you to do—ask him, and he will gladly tell you. He will not resent your asking.
>
> JAMES 1:5 NLT

On Parenting

If you're **careful** to
DISCIPLINE your children
when they're *young*, then
you won't have to **worry** about
them *so* much as they get older.

PROVERBS 22:6, PARAPHRASED

It's tempting to let toddlers and pre-schoolers get away with misbehavior because they're just so stinkin' cute. Unfortunately, that same behavior is not so adorable in an adolescent. It's much easier to shape and mold a young child than it is to try to retrain a teenager. Keep the long-term goal in sight, and make the investment of parenting your child right from the start. You'll enjoy the benefits for life. And they will enjoy the benefits of eternal life.

Week 1

Dear Lord, thank You for the privilege of parenting.
Strengthen me to be firm when it is the best way
to demonstrate my love. Show me how to teach my
children about You and Your ways, and keep my
children close to You all the days of their lives.

Dear Lord help me
to guide my children
to make good christian
decisions. It is so
very important that
each of our children
respect others. I
sometimes think my
expectations of them are
too high however I also
dont want to be too easy
with discipline. Dear
Lord please give me
strength to show my
children all of these
things while learning about you!

Today I will_____

_____

_____

_____

_____

_____

_____

_____

_____

_____

Train up a child in the WAY he should go;
even when he is old he will not **depart** from it.

PROVERBS 22:6

Wisdom in Action

13

On Peaceful Dinners

*I would rather eat leftovers
with a **PEACEFUL,** loving family
than *share* a table full of food
while **SURROUNDED** by
bickering and arguing.*

Proverbs 17:1, paraphrased

Have you ever noticed that when you're upset or anxious, your stomach gets all tied up in knots, and the last thing you feel like doing is eating? There's a direct correlation between stress and stomach problems. Don't you just hate it when a meal is spoiled because the kids are fighting or Dad is testy or you're tired and cranky? As moms we try hard to prepare delicious meals for our families to enjoy around the dinner table. I wonder if there's a way to put as much effort into the atmosphere around the table as we put into preparing the food that's on the table. I'll bet it would even make everything taste better.

Week 2

I want peace in our home. Jesus, since You are the
Prince of Peace, will You please reign in our family?
May the oil of Your spirit smooth the rough
edges around our relationships and conversations.
Where there is division, bring unity.

_____

_____

_____

_____

_____

_____

_____

_____

_____

_____

_____

_____

_____

_____

_____

Today I will_____

_____

_____

_____

_____

_____

_____

_____

_____

_____

_____

_____

Better is a dry morsel with **QUIET** than a house full of feasting with **strife**.

PROVERBS 17:1

Wisdom in Action

17

On Talking Too Much

The more you **talk,** the more likely you are to say SOMETHING you'll **regret** later. Hold your *tongue* and *think* before you speak.

PROVERBS 10:19, PARAPHRASED

Have you ever said to yourself, "When will I ever learn just to keep my mouth shut?!" We usually mutter this after we've been rambling on about something, not stopping until we've said too much. We need to go on a diet—a talking diet. Sure, it will be hard work, and it'll take a lot of discipline. Just as it's difficult to keep from opening our mouths to eat too much, it's equally hard to keep our mouths closed and not talk so much. But we can do it. And let's not wait until Monday to start.

Week 3

*God, give me the strength to keep my mouth closed
more often. Remind me of the wisdom of not saying
everything that comes to my mind. Since You say that
anything that flows out of our mouths
originates from the heart, perhaps I should ask
You to do a little cleansing of my "hearteries."*

_____

_____

_____

_____

_____

_____

_____

_____

_____

_____

_____

_____

_____

_____

On Talking Too Much

Today I will_____

_____

_____

_____

_____

_____

_____

_____

_____

_____

When *words* are many, **transgression** is not lacking, but whoever RESTRAINS his lips is *prudent*.

PROVERBS 10:19

Wisdom in Action

21

On Intentional Parenting

Does your child often **embarrass** you? Perhaps you've been lax with either **DISCIPLINING** the flesh or *teaching* the heart.

PROVERBS 29:15, PARAPHRASED

Balance, balance, balance.

If only parenting were as easy as simply spanking foolishness out of our children or talking them into making good choices. When we are most honest with ourselves, we have to admit that as moms we often have no idea what to do with our kids! Sometimes they drive us crazy and we feel like complete failures. But don't give up too soon. Remember, motherhood is a lifetime job. Just keep on disciplining your children when they make wrong choices and encouraging them when they choose wisely. Sometimes parenting calls for tough love, and sometimes we need to surprise our kids with grace and mercy. Ask their (heavenly) Father; He'll help you know what to do and when to do it.

Week 4

I need wisdom, Lord. I often feel totally helpless
when it comes to parenting. Whisper direction
to my heart so I'll know when my children need
a strong hand and when they need a gentle nudge.
I want to enjoy my kids.

_____

_____

_____

_____

_____

_____

_____

_____

_____

_____

_____

_____

_____

_____

_____

_____

Today I will_____

_____

_____

_____

_____

_____

_____

_____

_____

_____

The rod and reproof give **WISDOM,** but a child left to himself brings **shame** to his mother.

PROVERBS 29:15

Wisdom in Action

On Asking for Advice

It may **LOOK** like the right thing to do, and you may **think** you can see *everything* clearly, but it's still smarter to get another **PERSPECTIVE.**

PROVERBS 12:15, PARAPHRASED

You may have a great idea or know exactly how to accomplish something or have it all figured out. Or you could just be wrong and not be able to see it. As moms we've learned to be master problem solvers; but as capable as we are, we can't know everything all the time. Even when you think you've considered all the angles, don't let pride keep you from asking somebody else's opinion. Hey, if you're brilliant, it'll feel good to hear that from another person. On the other hand, if you're about to make a really stupid move, it would be good to find out now rather than later.

Week 5

Why is it that I always think my way is the right way? It may be fabulous, but it could always benefit from some improvement, right? Lord, train me to ask for other people's opinions, and give me a teachable spirit so I can receive constructive criticism and be open to opposing ideas.

_____

_____

_____

_____

_____

_____

_____

_____

_____

_____

_____

_____

_____

_____

Today I will _____

_____

_____

_____

_____

_____

_____

_____

_____

_____

_____

The way of a **fool** is right in his own eyes, but a **WISE** man listens to advice.

PROVERBS 12:15

Wisdom in Action

29

On Child Safety

If you trust **GOD** enough to obey Him, then you have **nothing** to worry about. Your *children* will also be safe because they'll **LEARN** to follow God's ways by **watching** you.

PROVERBS 14:26, PARAPHRASED

The "fear of the Lord" is an old-fashioned way of expressing awe and respect for who God is. He is the almighty God, Creator of the universe, the beginning and the end, Lord of lords and King of kings. As such, He is not to be taken lightly. Yes, He tells us we're His friends, but we are still wise to remember who He is—the great I Am. When we respectfully and humbly submit to His rightful authority in our lives, then we and our children are safe. It's when we start thinking we have the right to run our own lives that things get dangerous. When we take matters into our own hands and ignore God's wisdom, then, sadly, we're not the only ones who get hurt. Our children often pay the price for our rebellion as well.

Week 6

*Lord, help me to submit to Your authority in my life
and not fight You about who's going to be in control.
Remind me that godly authority in my life is a good
thing because it provides protection and covering.
Strengthen me to take my rightful place as the
God-given authority in my children's lives.*

_____

_____

_____

_____

_____

_____

_____

_____

_____

_____

_____

_____

_____

Wisdom to Pray

Today I will_____

_____

_____

_____

_____

_____

_____

_____

_____

_____

In the fear of the L*ORD* one has **strong** confidence, and his *children* will have a refuge.

PROVERBS 14:26

Wisdom in Action

On a Sharp Tongue

If you speak in the heat of **ANGER**,
you are going to **hurt** somebody.
If you're *smart*, you'll use your words
to **BUILD** up rather than **tear** down.

PROVERBS 12:18, PARAPHRASED

How many times have I hurt my children or other loved ones by saying something in anger? In the heat of the moment, I just have to speak, but I always feel terrible about it later. Unfortunately, it's too late then. The damage has already been done. I can apologize and restore the relationship, but I can't take back my words. I've learned the hard way that the best thing for me to do when I'm angry is to walk away and cool off. When I return, I can use my tongue to bring healing rather than pain.

Week 7

*God, please forgive me for the many times my
sharp words have hurt those I love. Help me to be
quick to apologize and to restore the relationship.
Speak to me of things I can say to others that will
bless their hearts and lives. I want my tongue
to be an instrument of healing.*

_____

_____

_____

_____

_____

_____

_____

_____

_____

_____

_____

_____

_____

_____

Today I will_____

_____

_____

_____

_____

_____

_____

_____

_____

_____

There is one whose rash WORDS are like sword thrusts, but the tongue of the **wise** brings *healing*.

PROVERBS 12:18

Wisdom in Action

37

On Seeking God

Wisdom for Today

You have to want to **KNOW** God more than **anything** else in the world. Worship Him and *actively* look for Him, and you **WILL** find Him.

PROVERBS 2:4–5, PARAPHRASED

If I offered you a parenting book that had all the answers you've ever wanted regarding how to raise the healthiest, happiest, and godliest children ever, would you devour that book, or would you leave it on the nightstand for days on end without picking it up? What if I gave you a map and told you that all you had to do was follow the directions on the map, grab a shovel, and dig deep, then you would surely find untold wealth; what would you do? I doubt you'd be too busy or think the map was too old to pay attention to or decide it wasn't worth the time and energy necessary to dig for it. And yet, too often, that's how we respond to the offer to know God and to find the wealth of wisdom He promises. Do we not think the opportunity to personally know the Creator of the universe is worth a little effort? I would think that having infinite wisdom available to us would be pretty valuable. You do too? Great—then pick up the nearest Bible and dig. There's treasure just waiting to be found.

Week 8

Oh, God, I do want to know You. Show me
where and how to find You. Make Your Word
come alive to me. Teach me to submit to You
as a trustworthy authority in my life. I want
nothing more in life than to find You.

_____

_____

_____

_____

_____

_____

_____

_____

_____

_____

_____

_____

_____

_____

_____

Today I will_____

_____

_____

_____

_____

_____

_____

_____

_____

_____

If you **SEEK** it like silver and **search** for it as for hidden *treasures,* then you will understand the **FEAR** of the LORD and *find* the knowledge of God.

PROVERBS 2:4–5

Wisdom in Action

On a Peaceful Home

A man would rather **LIVE**
by himself in a **shack** than
in a *mansion* with a woman who
is always **arguing** about something.

PROVERBS 21:9, PARAPHRASED

OK, ladies. Do you want your husband to stick around? Then stop fighting about everything. Every time you're tempted to say something you know is going to cause an argument, ask yourself: "Is the point I want to make really worth the friction it may cause?" I'm not saying you aren't probably right about whatever the issue is. I'm saying your husband doesn't care if you're right; he just wants to come home to some peace and quiet. Can you die to your rights and give him what he wants? Ultimately, you'll both win. And your children will win as they watch you treat your husband with love, humility, and respect. Ironically, losing is a win/win proposition. That's the way God works when we do things His way and trust Him with the results.

Week 9

Lord, I am so glad You're the Redeemer. Please
restore the brokenness in my marriage where
I've chipped away at the relationship with my
insistence on the way I think things should be.
Show me how to provide an atmosphere of
encouragement and acceptance in our home.

_____

_____

_____

_____

_____

_____

_____

_____

_____

_____

_____

_____

_____

_____

Today I will_____

_____

_____

_____

_____

_____

_____

_____

_____

_____

_____

_____

It is better to live in a CORNER of the housetop than in a house **shared** with a *quarrelsome* wife.

PROVERBS 21:9

Wisdom in Action

On Not Yelling

Wisdom for Today

Calm down and **SPEAK** softly.
The argument will only **escalate**
as you talk *louder* and attempt
to win by sheer **FORCE.**

PROVERBS 15:1, PARAPHRASED

It's amazing how potent a quiet response can be. Our motherly instincts tell us to talk louder and over our children to make sure we're heard. Our thinking goes something like this: *if they don't listen when I talk in a normal tone of voice, maybe they'll get it if I yell.* On top of that, our children are often arguing with us at the same time—so we feel as if we need to raise our voices to dominate the conversation. But the truth is, by simple physiology, a person has to listen more carefully to words spoken softly than to words that are shouted. Responding gently helps diffuse the anger so moms and kids can really hear each other's hearts. That's when true communication happens anyway.

Week 10

*Lord, please stop me in the middle of an argument
and calm me down long enough to get control of
my emotions. Remind me not to be as concerned
about winning the conflict as I am about gently
guiding the disagreement to a resolution.*

Today I will_____

_____

_____

_____

_____

_____

_____

_____

_____

_____

_____

_____

A soft answer **TURNS AWAY** wrath, but a harsh word **stirs up** anger.

PROVERBS 15:1

Wisdom in Action

On Independence

You can either do it **ALL** yourself and, in the end, **lose** it all, or you can *realize* from the beginning that you need help and **LET GOD** take care of you.

PROVERBS 15:25, PARAPHRASED

We can respond to God in two ways: We can try to impress Him by doing things in our own strength, attempting to be good enough, parenting in our own wisdom, and trying to prove that our way works. Or we can confess our vulnerability, admit our need, and depend on Him to take care of us and help us to be the moms we want to be. You might as well start with the second scenario because your heavenly Father cares too much about you to let you go your own way in your own strength. That always ends in disaster. Don't live in such a way that God has to tear down your "house," and you have to start over. Let Him build your life from the foundation.

Week 11

*Father, I admit that I'm needy, especially when it comes
to being a good mom. Please protect me, defend me, look
out for me, and take care of me. I can't do it all in my
own strength; I know that. Help me to always see clearly
Your awesomeness and my puniness so I'm not tempted
to walk in pride and independence.*

_____

_____

_____

_____

_____

_____

_____

_____

_____

_____

_____

_____

_____

_____

Today I will_____

_____

_____

_____

_____

_____

_____

_____

_____

_____

_____

_____

The LORD tears down the **house** of the proud but **MAINTAINS** the widow's boundaries.

PROVERBS 15:25

Wisdom in Action

On Tough Love

Children are not **naturally** good; they're **BORN** with evil hearts just *like* the rest of us. It's our **JOB** as parents to administer **tough** love when necessary to *teach* them right from wrong.

PROVERBS 22:15, PARAPHRASED

These days there's a big brou-haha about spanking. I don't have the desire or the space to get into that argument here. Let me just say this. If you, as a parent, can administer corporal punishment with love, wisdom, and self-control, then spanking can be an effective way to deal with rebellion. If, on the other hand, you believe corporal punishment is child abuse, then don't spank. The rod referred to in the Bible was an instrument for correction, but it also provided guidance and protection. Don't get hung up on "to spank or not to spank." Simply take up the rod of your authority, be the parent, and discipline your child. To do nothing would be child abuse indeed.

Week 12

Father, show me how to discipline my children effectively. Give me creative ideas to reach their hearts, where the real trouble begins. Reveal to me the best way to get through to each of my children with Your wisdom and ways.

Today I will_____

_____

_____

_____

_____

_____

_____

_____

_____

_____

_____

_____

Folly is *bound up* in the **heart** of a child,
but the rod of **DISCIPLINE** drives it far from him.

PROVERBS 22:15

Wisdom in Action

57

On Hearing God

If you listen to me **AND** obey me
when I **tell** you what to do, then
I will *continue* to speak to you
and **OPEN** your heart and ears
to **receive** my words.

PROVERBS 1:23, PARAPHRASED

When it comes to raising kids in today's world, we desperately need to hear from God. The truth is, we decide whether we hear from God or not. If He tells us a few simple things to do and we refuse to obey, is it any wonder when He stops speaking to us? If you haven't heard from God lately, go back to the last thing you know He said to you and do it. Are you going to church, reading your Bible, praying, and forgiving? These are just a few of the things God tells us to do. He's not asking us to jump through hoops. He just knows what makes life work for us. Trust Him. Obey Him. Then, rest assured, you will hear Him again.

Week 13

*Lord, I want to be quick to repent when You correct
me. Open my ears to hear You speak clear direction
to me through Your Spirit and by reading Your
Word. Remind me that it is Your power within
me that will enable me to overcome any weaknesses
You show me—and that You wouldn't point them
out if You didn't intend to help me.*

_____

_____

_____

_____

_____

_____

_____

_____

_____

_____

_____

_____

Today I will_____

_____

_____

_____

_____

_____

_____

_____

_____

_____

If you turn at my **REPROOF,** behold, I will pour out my *spirit* to you; I will make my words **known** to you.

PROVERBS 1:23

61

On Worry

Don't worry about **ANYTHING,**
and don't try to **figure** everything out.
If you keep your *focus* on simply
KNOWING GOD, He will make sure
everything turns out OK.

PROVERBS 3:5–6, PARAPHRASED

Telling a mom not to worry is like telling a child not to whine. I don't think it is possible. But we can certainly do our best to curb our anxieties. Start by choosing to believe that God is good all the time. Even when you can't figure out what He's up to in your life or when you simply don't know which way to turn or what to do. Turn to God and affirm, "You are my Lord, and I will obey You and trust You to take care of me." Then leave it to God to make a way. Submit all your hopes and dreams to Him. If they're part of His will, He will open the doors of opportunity. Don't try to attain them yourself. Your heavenly Father not only has the perfect plan for your life, but He also has the perfect timing.

Week 14

God, I love this Bible verse! It brings me such
comfort to know that I don't have to have it all
figured out. All I need to do is trust You and
allow You to be Lord of my life, and You'll take
care of the rest. Thank You, Lord.

_____

_____

_____

_____

_____

_____

_____

_____

_____

_____

_____

_____

_____

_____

_____

Today I will_____

_____

_____

_____

_____

_____

_____

_____

_____

Trust in the LORD with **ALL** your heart, and do not lean on **your own** understanding. In all your ways *acknowledge* him, and **HE WILL** make straight your paths.

PROVERBS 3:5–6

Wisdom in Action

65

On Keeping Your Mouth Shut

If you **DON'T KNOW** what you're **talking** about, then *keep* your mouth **SHUT,** and it won't be so *obvious*. People will **ASSUME** you do know, and they'll **give** you more *credit* than you deserve.

PROVERBS 17:28, PARAPHRASED

Try a little experiment. This week, whenever you find yourself talking with a group of people, try to say as little as possible, especially when it comes to parenting. Remember, your opinion is simply that—your opinion. We must remind ourselves to be merciful, understanding that what has worked for us and our families may not necessarily be the answer for someone else's family. Concentrate, instead, on listening. Not only will people think you're smarter than you really are, but you'll actually become wiser because you'll end up learning so much from others.

Week 15

Lord, teach me how to be a better listener.
Forgive me for the presumption of thinking I
need to offer my two-cents' worth in every
conversation. If I don't know what to say,
remind me that it's OK to say nothing.

_____

_____

_____

_____

_____

_____

_____

_____

_____

_____

_____

_____

_____

_____

Today I will _____

_____

_____

_____

_____

_____

_____

_____

_____

_____

Even a *fool* who keeps SILENT is considered wise; when he **closes** his lips, he is deemed intelligent.

PROVERBS 17:28

Wisdom in Action

69

On Keeping House

If you didn't have any **CHILDREN,**
your house would stay **cleaner**.
But there's *so* much **MORE** to life
than a **clean** house—like the
amazing *blessing* of family.

PROVERBS 14:4, PARAPHRASED

Just accept the fact that as long as you have children at home, your house is going to get messy. As soon as you get all the dishes washed, somebody's going to dirty another one. Caught up on all the laundry? Not for long. But what's really important—having everything in its place or spending time with your family? Every day you make a choice between the two. I'm not saying you shouldn't strive to have a neat house. Just don't sacrifice these short years when your children are at home for the lesser good of accomplishing everything on your to-do list. Some days let the dishes stack up and pull out a board game. Or forget vacuuming and go to the park instead. You may have to come home to a dirty house, but it's much better than coming home to an empty one.

Week 16

God, help me to get my priorities straight. Show me what's really important in this life. I do want to provide a clean and orderly home for my family, so show me how I can do that while also enjoying my home and family. Strengthen me to teach my children self-discipline so they can pitch in and help.

_____

_____

_____

_____

_____

_____

_____

_____

_____

_____

_____

_____

_____

_____

Today I will_____

_____

_____

_____

_____

_____

_____

_____

_____

_____

Where there are no **oxen,** the manger is clean, but *abundant* crops come by the **STRENGTH** of the ox.

PROVERBS 14:4

73

On Choosing Friends

You become like the **PEOPLE** you spend *time* with, and you may experience collateral **damage** by hanging out with the **WRONG** friends.

PROVERBS 13:20, PARAPHRASED

Choose your friends wisely. We've all heard that a million times. You've probably even said it to your own children at least a hundred times. Now it's time to listen to your own advice. Take a mental inventory of your friends. If you're smart, you'll make it a point to spend more time with people you admire. Look, too, at the lives of some of your friends that shouldn't be imitated. It's up to you to draw a line. Be there for them as a witness, but be careful not to let them influence you negatively, or you'll surely regret it. There's a fine line between being in the world but not of it.

Week 17

Lord, please bring good and godly friends into my life. If I'm spending time with people who will draw me away from You or cause me to stumble, give me the courage to walk away. Help me to pray for them but not set myself up for trouble by spending too much time with them. Jesus, I want You to be my best friend.

_____

_____

_____

_____

_____

_____

_____

_____

_____

_____

_____

_____

_____

Today I will_____

_____

_____

_____

_____

_____

_____

_____

_____

_____

Whoever walks with the WISE becomes wise, but the **companion** of *fools* will suffer harm.

PROVERBS 13:20

Wisdom in Action

77

On Living Simply

You will ultimately be **HAPPIER** with a **simple** life enjoyed without *compromise* than you would with having **MORE** than you'll ever need, **including** all the temptation and **STRESS** wealth *creates*.

PROVERBS 15:16, PARAPHRASED

Ask any rich person, and he or she will tell you that money won't make you happy. As a matter of fact, the stress and anxiety of keeping all that money and maintaining all that stuff can easily steal what joy you had in the first place. But we don't really want to hear that. We think if we could just have a bigger house or a car that doesn't always break down or a family vacation to Disney World, then we'd be satisfied. In reality, there will always be more stuff to want. The only thing that will truly satisfy is a personal relationship with the One who created us. If we have that, we'll be satisfied with very little—or, perhaps even more amazingly, content and not wanting even more when we have a whole lot.

Week 18

*God, open my eyes to see all of Your blessings around
me. Give me a grateful heart, and make me a
person who thanks You and praises You
often. Teach me to be content in any situation,
knowing that all I really need is You.*

Today I will_____

_____

_____

_____

_____

_____

_____

_____

_____

_____

_____

Better is a **little** with the FEAR of the LORD than great *treasure* and **trouble** with it.

PROVERBS 15:16

Wisdom in Action

81

On Nagging

Wisdom for Today

Nothing is quite as **annoying** as a constant drip or CONSTANT *complaining.* A husband **soon** discovers that it's FUTILE to try to **please** this kind of wife, so he just gives up and *tunes* her out.

PROVERBS 27:15–16, PARAPHRASED

Do you want to drive your man crazy? Then keep harping. I don't know what it is that you keep bringing up, but he surely does. And if he hasn't listened to you by now, saying it one more time isn't going to make him change. Same goes for dealing with our children, for that matter. Have you noticed that nagging doesn't actually work? If you must complain to somebody, take your frustrations to the Lord in prayer. He's always willing to listen, and He's actually able to make a change in your husband's and your children's hearts. (But He usually starts with ours.)

*God, I need help! I'm afraid I'm pushing my family
away with my dissatisfaction. Give me the faith to
believe that You will speak to them so I can shut up
about these complaints. Fill me with contentment
in You so I won't get so disappointed when I don't
feel fulfilled by my husband or as a mother.*

_____

_____

_____

_____

_____

_____

_____

_____

_____

_____

_____

_____

_____

_____

Today I will_____

_____

_____

_____

_____

_____

_____

_____

_____

$\mathscr{A}$ continual **DRIPPING** on a rainy day and a **quarrelsome** wife are alike; to restrain her is to *restrain* the wind or to grasp oil in one's right hand.

PROVERBS 27:15–16

Wisdom in Action

On Inconsistent Discipline

You show **LOVE** to your child by consistently **disciplining** him, not by *letting* him off the hook this time. That only **PROVES** you care more about **yourself** than you do about him.

PROVERBS 13:24, PARAPHRASED

Do you hate your child? Of course you don't. Then prove it by disciplining him. What? That certainly sounds backward. Today's culture tells us we should be best friends with our children and talk with them and encourage them to make good choices. That sounds good, and it may work—in an ideal world. I don't know about you, but my children don't always make the right choices, no matter how much I try to build up their self-esteem. Sometimes I just have to be the bad guy for their own good. They may not like me at that moment, but deep inside they'll know that I love them—enough to discipline them.

Heavenly Father, I love my children so much. Help me to be consistent in disciplining them. When I'm tired after a long day, don't let me succumb to the temptation to let things go that need to be dealt with. Give me a vision for the kind of heart responses from children that please You, and then help me not to stop praying and correcting until we reach that goal.

_____

_____

_____

_____

_____

_____

_____

_____

_____

_____

_____

_____

_____

Today I will_____

_____

_____

_____

_____

_____

_____

_____

_____

_____

Whoever spares the rod **HATES** his son, but he who *loves* him is **diligent** to discipline him.

PROVERBS 13:24

Wisdom in Action

89

On Motives

You can **JUSTIFY** anything to anyone **but** God. He can see straight through to the *real* reasons **BEHIND** your actions.

PROVERBS 21:2, PARAPHRASED

It is so easy to rationalize our choices and behavior. If we want to do something badly enough, we can certainly come up with justification for getting our way. (Sound like any munchkins around your house?) We may not even recognize our wrong motives. It's entirely possible that we sincerely believe we're doing the right things for the right reasons. That's why it's critical that we give God full access to our hearts and lives. We must submit all of our ways to Him and ask Him to search our hearts for any selfishness that may unwittingly creep in.

Week 21

I can get away with a lot and outsmart plenty of
people. But not You, Lord. You know why I do
things. You see when I'm really doing a good thing
because I have something to gain by being nice.
Since You can see my heart so clearly, and I'm often
blind to my own impure motives, please open my
eyes to my honest (or not-so-honest) intentions.

_____

_____

_____

_____

_____

_____

_____

_____

_____

_____

_____

_____

_____

Today I will_____

_____

_____

_____

_____

_____

_____

_____

_____

_____

_____

_____

Every way of a man is RIGHT in his own eyes, but the LORD **weighs** the heart.

PROVERBS 21:2

Wisdom in Action

93

On Being in Control

If you can **CONTROL** your temper,
you're **already** ahead of the game.
And if you have *self-discipline*,
there will be **NO** stopping you.

PROVERBS 16:32, PARAPHRASED

If two people are arguing, and one person is shouting and the other one is calm, which one do you think is winning? Which one do you think is the mother, and which one is the child? Ouch. If one of you is "putting the other person in her place" with harsh and cruel words, and the other person has thought of a few choice words to say but chooses to keep them to herself, who do you think is more powerful? We cannot let ourselves be reduced to our children's level by acting immaturely and entering into a shouting match with them. We'll never win the argument or, more importantly, their respect by controlling them with our tone of voice. Appearances can be deceiving, so if you really want to be strong, choose to be weak. Calmly suggest to your child that you continue the discussion when both of you have had a chance to calm down. You may even want to resume the conversation by beginning with a prayer, seeking the Lord for His help to resolve the issue.

Week 22

God, I want to be strong enough to lay down my arms in the heat of the battle, knowing that You will fight for me. Help me get to the cause of this anger within me that rears its ugly head so readily. Strengthen my spirit to overcome this weakness.

_____

_____

_____

_____

_____

_____

_____

_____

_____

_____

_____

_____

_____

_____

Today I will_____

_____

_____

_____

_____

_____

_____

_____

_____

_____

_____

Whoever is **SLOW** to anger is better than the mighty, and he who **rules** his spirit than he who takes a city.

PROVERBS 16:32

Wisdom in Action

97

On Taking Responsibility

It is not OK to **IRRESPONSIBLY HURT** someone, **not** thinking about how he or she might *feel*, and **ASSUME** you can **make** it all better by *saying,* "I was only **kidding**!"

PROVERBS 26:18–19, PARAPHRASED

My children do this all the time, and it drives me crazy. I came to the point where I finally had to tell my son, "If you have to say, 'I was just kidding' after you've done something, you should probably just follow it up with, 'I'm sorry I hurt you.'" Sometimes what's in our hearts slips out without our realizing it. We think we can recover by pretending we were joking. But it's too late. The damage has been done. If you find this happening far too often, you may want to ask the Lord to get inside and perform some open-heart surgery.

Week 23

God, forgive me for saying and doing things I regret
and then trying to cover them up and make things
better with a simple, "Just joking!" Help me to at
least have the guts to admit when I've made a
mistake and the courage to ask for forgiveness.

_____

_____

_____

_____

_____

_____

_____

_____

_____

_____

_____

_____

_____

_____

_____

Today I will_____

_____

_____

_____

_____

_____

_____

_____

_____

_____

Like a madman who **THROWS** firebrands,
arrows, and **death** is the man who *deceives*
his neighbor and says, "I am only **JOKING!**"

PROVERBS 26:18–19

Wisdom in Action

On Fear

God's character is trustworthy.
When you are afraid, **DEPEND** on
Him to take **care** of you.

PROVERBS 18:10, PARAPHRASED

You've heard the phrase "A good name is more valuable than . . ." A person's name is closely linked with his or her reputation. When the Bible refers to "the name of the LORD," it's referring to God's character. The name of the Lord is good, holy, righteous, merciful, patient, slow to anger, and all-powerful, to name a few. Because the Lord's character is so solid, we can trust that He will never let us down. He's a safe bet. When you feel the pressures of life closing in on you, fix your eyes on the Lord, run directly for Him, and cry, "Safe!"

Week 24

Lord, sometimes I worry about everything. Am I being
too strict? Too lenient? Too busy? Too lazy? Are my
kids going to be safe? Is my husband going
to lose his job? Am I a complete failure as a mother?
It can get overwhelming. The next time I find
myself burdened under stress and anxiety, remind
me to run to You. You are strong enough, good enough,
powerful enough, and loving enough to take care
of all my worries. Help me to trust You.

_____

_____

_____

_____

_____

_____

_____

_____

_____

_____

_____

Today I will _____

_____

_____

_____

_____

_____

_____

_____

_____

_____

_____

_____

The name of the **LORD** is a strong tower; the **righteous** man runs into it and is *safe*.

PROVERBS 18:10

Wisdom in Action

On Being Full of Hot Air

A fool isn't really **LISTENING** to
what **YOU** have to say because he already
thinks he knows it all. He just
loves the **SOUND** of his *own* voice.

PROVERBS 18:2, PARAPHRASED

Wisdom for Today

It's easy to get so focused on getting our point across or winning an argument or proving ourselves right that we forget the far more worthy goal is to understand the truth. And the truth is, it's hard to balance being moms who know best with being good listeners who don't always know it all. A conversation should be a two-way exchange, like playing catch. Yet, too often it looks more like handball—and this doesn't just happen with our kids. We act as though the other person's role in the game were simply to be a sounding board for us to express our own views. The whole time the other person is talking, we're busy thinking about how we're going to respond, rather than truly listening. How boring! Any game is more fun with two players.

Week 25

God, I don't want to be a fool, and yet I often act like one. I really do want to learn and grow. Help me to find more pleasure in hearing other people's points of view than in expressing my own. Forgive me for the pride that leads me to think everyone wants to hear what I have to say.

_____

_____

_____

_____

_____

_____

_____

_____

_____

_____

_____

_____

_____

_____

Today I will_____

_____

_____

_____

_____

_____

_____

_____

_____

_____

_____

A fool takes no pleasure in understanding,
but only in **expressing** his *opinion*.

PROVERBS 18:2

Wisdom in Action

On Tattletales

Don't be too **QUICK** to make a judgment. Make **sure** you hear *both* sides of the story.

PROVERBS 18:17, PARAPHRASED

As a mom, do you ever feel like a part-time referee? Or perhaps judge and jury? Moms also need to be pretty good lawyers. I don't know about your kids, but mine don't always volunteer the whole truth and nothing but the truth. As mothers we have to listen to both sides of the argument, ask the right questions, and look at the evidence. It would be so much quicker and easier if we could simply cast our verdicts based on circumstantial evidence and motherly instinct rather than hear all the long, drawn-out testimonies of arguing siblings. But our children deserve better. Granted, life isn't fair, but they need to know that Mom is.

I need patience; give it to me now! I'm only half kidding, Lord. I do and say things I regret because I get so easily irritated with my children. Refresh me with peace, joy, and patience with my little ones. Help me to take the time to listen to them carefully and ask them questions that show I really do care about what they're thinking and feeling.

_____

_____

_____

_____

_____

_____

_____

_____

_____

_____

_____

_____

Today I will _____

_____

_____

_____

_____

_____

_____

_____

_____

_____

_____

_____

_____

The one who states his case **FIRST** seems right, **until** the other comes and examines him.

PROVERBS 18:17

Wisdom in Action

On Comparison Shopping

FANTASIZING about another man is **tantalizing,** but even entertaining the *thought* can bring DEATH to a marriage.

PROVERBS 9:17–18, PARAPHRASED

114

I know the grass always looks greener on the other side. I'm sure you've met other men who appear to be just what you need in a husband. Maybe they really listen to you. It could be that they simply appear to be more interested in you than your own husband is. Or perhaps they look like the spiritual leader you've always wanted in your home. They could even be incredible dads. It doesn't matter! Even if they truly have all of these wonderful qualities (they probably don't, and I can guarantee they have plenty of irritating traits that are just temporarily concealed), the bottom line is that fantasizing about them (not to mention acting on your fantasies) is like taking a bite of a poisoned apple. It may be juicy and sweet, but the end result is death. Think—would it really be worth it? No? Then stop even thinking about it.

Week 27

God, purify my thoughts. Do whatever housecleaning is necessary regarding the influences I let into my mind and heart, whether through media choices or friends. Snatch me away from the devil if he begins to seduce me into looking to anything or anyone other than You. Save me, Lord.

_____

_____

_____

_____

_____

_____

_____

_____

_____

_____

_____

_____

_____

Today I will_____

_____

_____

_____

_____

_____

_____

_____

_____

Wisdom in Action

"*Stolen* water tastes best, and the food you eat in **SECRET** tastes best of all." None who listen to Stupidity **understand** that her guests are as good as dead.

PROVERBS 9:17–18 CEV

On Consideration

Give your **FRIENDS** some **BREATHING** room. Don't become clingy, or they may get **tired** of your *always* being around and resent you for it.

PROVERBS 25:17, PARAPHRASED

In this day and age we probably don't spend enough time at our neighbors' houses. Everybody is always busy. But the crazy schedules that keep us isolated from each other also mean we need to be careful not to overstay our welcome when we do visit. It's probably a good idea to begin even a phone conversation with, "Is this a good time to talk?" We need to be considerate of others' time, even when our children run over to a friend's house to play. It's easy to lose track of time when our children are happily and safely occupied, but we must be careful not to let them "live" at someone else's house, even if they are best friends.

Week 28

Lord, I want friends, and I want to be a good friend.
Teach me to be the kind of friend who fills others up
rather than sucks them dry. Help me to balance my
desire to reach out and be friendly with being sensitive
to other people's needs and schedules. And help me teach
my children that kind of sensitivity and consideration.

_____

_____

_____

_____

_____

_____

_____

_____

_____

_____

_____

_____

_____

_____

Today I will_____

_____

_____

_____

_____

_____

_____

_____

_____

_____

_____

_____

Let your foot be **seldom** in your neighbor's house, lest he have his **FILL** of you and hate you.

PROVERBS 25:17

Wisdom in Action

121

On Good Works

God would **RATHER** you simply
live **right** and *think* of others
than try to **IMPRESS** Him with how hard
you're working by *doing* stuff for Him.

PROVERBS 21:3, PARAPHRASED

We can teach a Sunday School class, lead a Bible study, sing in the choir, homeschool our kids, give up high-salary careers to spend more time with our families, and still our hearts can be far from the Lord. That's why God is more pleased when we simply trust Him and obey Him than when we do a bunch of good works. He would rather see us reach out to our neighbor and care for the poor than be in church every time the doors are open. Remember, God isn't interested in religion. He wants a relationship.

Wisdom for Living

Week 29

God, I know I can't gain Your approval or get into heaven by way of my good works. It's only because Jesus paid the price for my sin by dying on the cross and conquering death through His resurrection that I can be forgiven. It's only by the righteousness You give me as a free gift that allows me the privilege of relationship with You. Thank You that by my accepting Jesus as my savior, You accept me as Your child.

_____

_____

_____

_____

_____

_____

_____

_____

_____

_____

_____

Today I will_____

_____

_____

_____

_____

_____

_____

_____

_____

_____

_____

To do righteousness and **JUSTICE** is more **acceptable** to the LORD than *sacrifice.*

PROVERBS 21:3

Wisdom in Action

On Boasting

Don't toot your **OWN** horn.
Let somebody **else** brag
about how *great* you are.

PROVERBS 27:2, PARAPHRASED

As moms we do a lot for our families and for others. And it's great when others recognize all the wonderful things about us and appreciate the sacrifices we're making. But if they don't notice, it's tempting to point out those things ourselves. Unfortunately, this tends to have the opposite of the desired effect: not only do others not praise us for our accomplishments, but they often feel the need to humble us and remind us of our place. Now, you and I know that recognition of our efforts is less a matter of pride than it is the need to feel appreciated. Maybe the solution is to remember that God sees everything we do, and He loves us unconditionally. His opinion is the most important one anyway. If someone else notices and comments, that's just a bonus.

Week 30

*I really like approval, Lord. It makes me feel good
when people think I'm special. Help me not to be so
desperate for attention that I have to go after it myself.
From a place of confidence in Your love for me, help me
to look for ways to praise other people, understanding
how powerful encouraging words can be.*

_____

_____

_____

_____

_____

_____

_____

_____

_____

_____

_____

_____

Today I will_____

_____

_____

_____

_____

_____

_____

_____

_____

_____

_____

Wisdom in Action

Let another **PRAISE** you, and not your own mouth; a stranger, and **not** your *own* lips.

Proverbs 27:2

On Tithes and Offerings

The ABUNDANCE you have
has been **given** to you by the Lord,
so keep it coming by *returning*
to Him your **BEST** off the top.
Then **acknowledge** Him with a grateful
heart for the ability to *enjoy* the rest.

PROVERBS 3:9–10, PARAPHRASED

Raising children and running a household bring what can feel like endless expenses, and sometimes it can feel like a strain on our budgets to give tithes and offerings. But here's the bottom line: we're not giving *our* money to God; we are returning to Him a portion of what He has given to us. Talk about a good investment! He says that if we give big, we'll get big. If we're stingy, we won't have much to give anyway. God doesn't need our money. He's simply looking to see if we really are going to trust Him with our finances. Are we willing to play by His rules? If we are, we can't lose. He'll make sure we win—by a lot.

Week 31

God, help me to live openhandedly so that I not
only may bless others but also may be open to
receive more directly from Your hand of abundance.
I want to be a cheerful giver. Give me the
courage to trust Your ways by giving away
money and relying on You to take care of me.

_____

_____

_____

_____

_____

_____

_____

_____

_____

_____

_____

_____

_____

_____

Today I will_____

_____

_____

_____

_____

_____

_____

_____

_____

Honor the LORD with **YOUR** wealth and with the **firstfruits** of all your produce; then your barns will be filled with *plenty*, and your vats will be **BURSTING** with wine.

PROVERBS 3:9–10

Wisdom in Action

On Leaving a Godly Heritage

If you live an **UPRIGHT** life before the Lord and people, then **even** your *children* will enjoy the blessings.

Proverbs 20:7, paraphrased

It would be great to leave our children a large inheritance. Hey, it would be nice simply to save enough to pay for their college education. We spend enormous time and energy providing for our kids and working to supply all of their needs—and as many wants as possible. Sadly, we sometimes even compromise on other important things in order to give them all we can. We may work way too many hours away from home or make questionable decisions or cut moral corners because everyone else does. We forget that one of the best things we can give our children is a good name. Our kids have a better shot at happiness if we make our choices based on an eternal perspective rather than on temporary pleasures.

Week 32

*Lord, thank You for Your promises to us when we
obey You and follow Your ways. Thank you that
we are not the only ones who benefit from our
decision to trust You. Pour out Your blessings on
my children. Show them that in following You
there is safety, peace, abundance, and joy.*

On Leaving a Godly Heritage

Today I will_____

_____

_____

_____

_____

_____

_____

_____

_____

_____

_____

The righteous who walks in his **integrity**
—blessed are his **CHILDREN** after him!

PROVERBS 20:7

On Weighing Your Words

Be careful what you **SAY**, because
you may have to **eat** your words later.
Will those **WORDS** come back to *bite* you,
or will they **GO** down easy?

PROVERBS 18:21, PARAPHRASED

Moms are powerful! We wield quite a bit of influence, not only by virtue of our position, but also by the depth of understanding and love we have for our families. Whether we want to admit it or not, the things we say have the potential to change the course of others' lives— our family members', our friends', and even our own. When those we love are nearby, we wouldn't casually swing around a sharp sword; someone might get hurt. Words can be just as cutting, yet we're often not careful at all with the things we say. God created the world with His words. We, too, can bring life—or death—with our words. We need to be careful and be intentional.

Week 33

God, I need to be more careful with the offhanded remarks I make. They can do more damage than I ever intended. As You remind me to choose my words wisely, help me to purposely speak words that will change people's lives for the better.

_____

_____

_____

_____

_____

_____

_____

_____

_____

_____

_____

_____

_____

_____

_____

_____

Today I will_____

_____

_____

_____

_____

_____

_____

_____

_____

_____

_____

_____

Death and **LIFE** are in the power of the tongue, and those who **love** it will eat its fruits.

PROVERBS 18:21

Wisdom in Action

On Hard Times

Don't get **UPSET** with God or give up when **hard** times come. It's **because** your heavenly Father *cares* so much about you that He **ALLOWS** tough circumstances to **shape** your character.

PROVERBS 3:11–12, PARAPHRASED

Most of us can admit we aren't perfect. So why are we surprised when we go through difficult circumstances? God uses tough times to shape us and mold us into the people He created us to be. He loves us just the way we are, but that doesn't mean He's going to accept anything but the best for—and from—us. He wants us to be all we can be, not just as moms but as individuals. And that's not going to happen without a little pain. Instead of trying to figure out the fastest way to avoid difficulties, let's ask God to walk beside us as we go through the tough times. He'll bring us through to the other side better because of the suffering. Our heavenly Father adores us, and He cares for us too much to let us take the easy way out.

Week 34

*Father, because I know that You are a loving parent
and that anything You require of me is for my own
good, I can delight even in correction. Help me
not to resist change but to cooperate with the
adjustments You want to make in me. Thanks for
loving me enough to patiently teach me.*

_____

_____

_____

_____

_____

_____

_____

_____

_____

_____

_____

_____

_____

Today I will_____

_____

_____

_____

_____

_____

_____

_____

_____

_____

_____

Do not despise the LORD's **DISCIPLINE** or be weary of his **reproof,** for the LORD reproves him whom he *loves*.

PROVERBS 3:11–12

145

On Self-Control

If you can't **CONTROL** your passions, you'll be **vulnerable** to the enemy's *attack* and to possible **BONDAGE**.

PROVERBS 25:28, PARAPHRASED

We've all seen it. Lives destroyed by addictions. Marriages dissolved because of unbridled lust or anger. Children in trouble because they've never been disciplined. A lack of self-control can rob and defeat any life. Even "acceptable" indulgences, like overeating, hasty spending, or unholy media choices, can leave us open to attack. Yet self-control is listed as a fruit of the Spirit. That tells us we can't be strong enough on our own. We need help from the Spirit of God to control our impulses, even our less passionate ones. Thankfully, that power is available. All we need is enough self-control to ask for it.

Week 35

OK, Lord, I really need Your help in this area. Many parts of my life are broken down because of my lack of self-control. My prayer is that You will strengthen me from the inside out and then restore and redeem those things I've lost because of my sin. Bring healing where there has been destruction.

_____

_____

_____

_____

_____

_____

_____

_____

_____

_____

_____

_____

_____

_____

Today I will_____

_____

_____

_____

_____

_____

_____

_____

_____

_____

_____

_____

$\mathcal{A}$ man without **SELF-CONTROL** is like a city **broken** into and left without walls.

PROVERBS 25:28

Wisdom in Action

On Apathy

Don't just **STAND** back and plead ignorance as you **watch** innocent people die. Get in there and *help* them.

PROVERBS 24:11, PARAPHRASED

As moms we're so busy taking care of our families' needs that it's easy look past the needs of people outside that circle. But God tells us we're responsible for others too. Look around. Who needs your help? Are there any neglected elderly people, unwanted babies, or abandoned children who could use your intervention? Have you visited the inner city lately? What about the streets of downtown? Our lives are so incredibly blessed, couldn't we give just a little of our time and resources to help those less fortunate? Begin checking with organizations in your city that help those who can't help themselves, and volunteer to do whatever they need. You may be surprised at how much you get by giving.

Week 36

God, show me where I can make a difference in my community. Give me a swift kick in the pants when I start becoming myopic in my view of the world. Open my eyes to see the needs around me, and then give me Your vision for what I can do to help. Use me, Lord!

Today I will_____

_____

_____

_____

_____

_____

_____

_____

_____

_____

_____

Rescue those who are being **TAKEN** away to **death;** hold back those who are **STUMBLING** to the slaughter.

PROVERBS 24:11

Wisdom in Action

153

On Gossip

Wisdom for Today

If someone is **SHARING** a juicy **tidbit** with you about somebody else, rest assured they're *also* talking about you **BEHIND** your back. Stay away from **this** kind of "friend."

PROVERBS 20:19, PARAPHRASED

$\mathcal{A}$ *good rule* of thumb is, if someone gossips *to* you, she'll probably also gossip *about* you. But what can we do when we're caught in a situation where gossip is being handed to us? First, we can try to graciously change the subject or turn a conversation headed in a negative direction around with a positive spin. For example, if one mom starts "commenting" on another mom's parenting skills or housekeeping finesse or playing any other comparison game, take the opportunity to point out something good about the mom in question. If the speaker doesn't catch the subtle hint, you may need to come right out and say you'd rather not talk about other people. But if the person persists, it may be time to look for a new friend.

Week 37

Lord, sometimes it's fun to talk about other people.
It's easy to get caught up in that kind of conversation.
But I know it's wrong. Help me not to be the kind
of person who repeats gossip, and show me how
to turn conversations in a better direction when
someone else is tempted to spread rumors.

Today I will_____

_____

_____

_____

_____

_____

_____

_____

_____

_____

_____

Wisdom in Action

Whoever goes about SLANDERING reveals secrets; **therefore** do not associate with a simple *babbler*.

PROVERBS 20:19

On Living a Life of Integrity

If you live your life in the **LIGHT**, **understanding** that God sees everything, then you can *relax* and stop **WORRYING** about your **SECRET** sins being *discovered*.

PROVERBS 10:9, PARAPHRASED

I like to define integrity as living your life as though no one but God was watching. Sometimes that means I could get away with a secret sin, but I choose not to because I don't want to displease God. Other times it means I choose to please God even if that upsets people I care about. If we live our lives before an audience of One, then we can rest easy as long as we know He's happy. As moms it helps to remember that besides the "Big Eye in the Sky," little eyes are constantly focused on our every choice. Our children will reflect what we model before them. I don't want to be embarrassed if someday they reflect my "at home" behavior when we're not at home.

Week 38

*God, please shine a searchlight on my heart and
expose any hidden sins. I want to bring them into the
light of Your love so I can be forgiven and cleansed.
Keep my conscience sensitive so I won't tolerate any
hint of shadow in my thoughts or actions.*

_____

_____

_____

_____

_____

_____

_____

_____

_____

_____

_____

_____

_____

_____

On Living a Life of Integrity

Today I will_____

_____

_____

_____

_____

_____

_____

_____

_____

_____

Whoever walks in INTEGRITY walks securely, but he who makes his ways **crooked** will be *found* out.

PROVERBS 10:9

On Revenge

Don't take **MATTERS** into your **own** hands. Be *patient;* God will **EVEN** the score.

PROVERBS 20:22, PARAPHRASED

It's human nature to want revenge. When someone wrongs us—or especially our children—everything within us rises up and demands justice. Yet God tells us not to seek revenge. He isn't saying that the other person doesn't deserve to pay for what he or she did. He's simply telling us to let Him handle it. If we take the law into our own hands, we'll more than likely end up doing or saying something that demands justice be met against us. The best thing to do is to leave justice to the Authority. But we needn't worry; He's perfectly capable of defending us and our families.

Week 39

Father, thank You for not giving me what I deserve.
If I had to pay for all the bad things I've done and
the hurt I've caused, my situation would be hopeless.
When someone hurts me or my family, help me to hand
them over to You. And should You choose to show them
mercy, as You do me, then help me to trust You.

_____

_____

_____

_____

_____

_____

_____

_____

_____

_____

_____

_____

_____

Today I will_____

_____

_____

_____

_____

_____

_____

_____

_____

_____

_____

Do not say, "I will **REPAY** evil"; wait for the LORD, and he will **deliver** you.

PROVERBS 20:22

Wisdom in Action

On Working Hard

Doing as **LITTLE** as possible to get by will **get** you as little as possible. But if you're *faithful* day in **AND** day out, you will ultimately have **all** you need and more.

PROVERBS 10:4, PARAPHRASED

Now this is just common sense. If we're lazy and not willing to work hard, we aren't going to accomplish much. But if we don't give up, if we keep doing a good job, even on those days when we're tired of working and bored with our lives, then we will be rewarded. I'm not just talking about monetary rewards. As moms we put in long, exhausting hours, and the result is that we get to enjoy the richness of a loving family in a peaceful home with happy kids. That makes it all worthwhile.

Week 40

Lord, would You please allow me to do work I enjoy?
Help me to find fulfillment in using the gifts You've
placed within me. I want to experience deep satisfaction
in working hard. During those times when I'm not so
thrilled about my job as a mom, help me to perform it as
unto You and to find joy in pleasing You.

_____

_____

_____

_____

_____

_____

_____

_____

_____

_____

_____

_____

_____

_____

Today I will_____

_____

_____

_____

_____

_____

_____

_____

_____

_____

_____

_____

A slack hand causes **POVERTY,** but the hand of the **diligent** makes rich.

PROVERBS 10:4

Wisdom in Action

On Bad Habits

As DISGUSTING as it is,
if you're **addicted** to a sin,
you do the same *nauseating*
things over AND over again.

PROVERBS 26:11, PARAPHRASED

Why do we keep making the same mistakes? We promise ourselves we'll do better next time. We vow to overcome. We try as hard as we can . . . only to eventually fall again. What would make us return to that which made us sick in the first place? We are human, we are sinners, and without the grace of God, we are fools destined for a life of foolishness. Our only hope is in Jesus and the power He gives us to live an overcoming life. We also need a few good friends. We must be willing to come clean and admit our weaknesses to someone else who will commit to pray with us and for us and who loves us enough to tell us when we're acting like a dog returning to its vomit. Gross.

Week 41

Lord, come in power and deliver me from my sin! You know the area of my life where, as hard as I try, as sincere as my resolve is, I continue to fail. I admit it. I can't overcome this on my own. I'm calling out to You, in the mighty name of Jesus, and asking You to win this battle for me. I'm desperate, Lord. Please help me.

Today I will_____

_____

_____

_____

_____

_____

_____

_____

_____

_____

_____

_____

Like a dog that returns to his **VOMIT** is a fool who **repeats** his folly.

PROVERBS 26:11

On Playing Dumb

For your own **GOOD,** don't get
so upset over every **little** offense.
Some things it's just *better* to ignore
and **PRETEND** they never happened.

PROVERBS 19:11, PARAPHRASED

We have a saying in our house: "Just let it go." Usually it's directed toward siblings in conflict, but I find myself needing to heed this advice just as often. I'm so focused on consistently correcting and training my children that I sometimes disobey God's reminder not to exasperate them. I would love to say that I only have this problem when dealing with my children, but I also have to be careful with others in my life. In this world there are many things worth getting upset about, but there are far more that we should simply ignore. We don't have to demand justice at every slight. There's no need to be proven right just because we think someone else is wrong. Sometimes problems just happen, and no one is to blame. Relax, get over it—let it go!

Week 42

God, I don't want the little things to bug me so much. I want to see the big picture from Your perspective of what's important. Perform a deep work in me so I'm not so quick to flare up in anger. Fill me with Your mercy so I can be quick to forgive rather than demand justice.

_____

_____

_____

_____

_____

_____

_____

_____

_____

_____

_____

_____

_____

Today I will_____

_____

_____

_____

_____

_____

_____

_____

_____

_____

_____

Good sense makes one **SLOW** to anger, and it is his glory to **overlook** an offense.

PROVERBS 19:11

Wisdom in Action

177

On Financial Planning

Take good **CARE** of what
you have now, but **also** think
ahead and *plan* for the future.

PROVERBS 27:23–24, PARAPHRASED

I hate the word budget, don't you? I know a budget is important and, ultimately, a good thing. But I'd still rather not have to think about how much money I do or don't have. Still, it's important to know what kind of condition our finances are in. We do need to take saving for the future seriously. Who knows whether our family will be one of the next to face unemployment? Life carries no guarantees. Thankfully, our hope is in the Lord, not in our financial security. Yes, we should plan for the future, but we should never forget that the future is in God's hands.

Week 43

I want to be a good steward of the resources You've given me, Lord. Show me the balance between enjoying the abundance You love to give and being wasteful and materialistic. Teach me how to be wise about planning for the future without trusting in myself rather than You for security.

_____

_____

_____

_____

_____

_____

_____

_____

_____

_____

_____

_____

_____

_____

Today I will_____

_____

_____

_____

_____

_____

_____

_____

_____

_____

Know well the **CONDITION** of your flocks, and give **attention** to your herds, for riches do not last *forever;* and does a crown **ENDURE** to all generations?

PROVERBS 27:23–24

Wisdom in Action

On Confession

Don't just try to **HIDE** your sin
and **act** like it *never* happened.
Come clean and **DEAL** with it,
and then God will be able to **help** you.

Proverbs 28:13, paraphrased

We may think we're getting away with sin, but we never really do. Try as we may to hide it, it always rears its ugly head some way or another—even if that simply means robbing us of a clear conscience or blocking the flow of blessings. The best thing to do is bring the darkness into the light of Jesus. As moms we're so used to holding our kids accountable that we forget we need to be accountable too. Find a trustworthy friend and admit you're having trouble. Believe me, friends have weak areas too, so they won't think terrible things about you. As a matter of fact, they'll probably think more highly of you for having the courage to deal with your sin. Ask God to help you make any changes in your life that are necessary. And give your friend permission to ask you blunt questions occasionally as a point of accountability. Two are definitely better than one, and it's hard to beat the strength of three.

Week 44

Thank You, Lord, for the privilege of forgiveness.
I can't believe Your mercy is available to me no
matter what I've done, and all I have to do is ask.
Give me good friends I can turn to for help. Most
of all, I ask for Your help to turn from my past
and walk into the future You have for me.

_____

_____

_____

_____

_____

_____

_____

_____

_____

_____

_____

_____

_____

_____

Today I will_____

_____

_____

_____

_____

_____

_____

_____

_____

_____

_____

Whoever CONCEALS his transgressions will not prosper, but he who **confesses** and forsakes them will obtain *mercy*.

PROVERBS 28:13

185

On the Will of God

Be prepared and **DO** everything you can to do a **good** job, but ultimately, whether you *succeed* is up to the Lord.

PROVERBS 21:31, PARAPHRASED

It's right and good to work hard. As moms we want to do the best we can at the responsibilities God has entrusted to us. We play a big part in whether our lives, and the lives of our children, are victorious. So we must be self-disciplined and alert and always growing stronger. We must train our children and teach them and pray for them. But the end result is up to God. We can do all of the right things from the outside in, but only God can work from the inside out. And that's where real success is determined—in the heart.

Lord, I want to be ready. I want to be found
faithful. But I also want to be a woman
of faith, trusting that You can win the battle
regardless of how hard I try. Help me to
believe more in You than I do in my own
strength so that I might have faith for mighty
victories in my life and in my family.

_____

_____

_____

_____

_____

_____

_____

_____

_____

_____

_____

_____

On the Will of God

Today I will_____

_____

_____

_____

_____

_____

_____

_____

_____

_____

_____

_____

The horse is made **ready** for the day of battle, but the **VICTORY** belongs to the LORD.

PROVERBS 21:31

Wisdom in Action

189

On Taking Care of the Poor

If you ignore the **NEEDS** of others, don't expect any **help** from God when *you* need it.

PROVERBS 21:13, PARAPHRASED

Sure, we can close our eyes to the needs around us. After all, we have our hands full taking care of our own families. We figure that what we don't know won't hurt us, and better yet, we won't be held accountable for our ignorance. Think again. If we decide not to acknowledge the desperate needs around the globe, what we choose not to know will eventually hurt us. The day will come when we need help, and our cries will be ignored. As moms our hearts are already tuned to taking care of the vulnerable and needy. Let's take this sensitivity one step further and reach beyond our own children. Better yet, let's bring our children along and model reaching out to others in the name and image of God.

Week 46

*Father, forgive me for being so concerned about myself
and my problems that I've ignored the cries of those all
around me. Give me a big heart, like Yours, that cares
deeply about those who are hurting and in need. I've
enjoyed the benefits of Your generous heart; allow me
the privilege of sharing that giving spirit with others.*

_____

_____

_____

_____

_____

_____

_____

_____

_____

_____

_____

_____

_____

On Taking Care of the Poor

Today I will_____

_____

_____

_____

_____

_____

_____

_____

_____

_____

_____

Whoever closes his ear to the CRY of the poor will **himself** call out and not be answered.

PROVERBS 21:13

Wisdom in Action

On Walking Away from a Fight

It's easier to clean up a **DROP** of water than a **flood.** By the same token, it's *wiser* to drop an argument **BEFORE** it turns into a **full-fledged** fight.

PROVERBS 17:14, PARAPHRASED

It starts with a little dig or a nasty remark or an accusation. At that moment, each of us has a choice. Am I going to respond to this, knowing where that road leads? Or am I going to ignore it and head off a fight before it even starts? Let's take a minute and learn from our own preaching . . . uh, I mean lecturing . . . uh, I mean character training. What are we always saying to our children when they start bickering and fighting? From a mother's perspective, what does it look like when our kids argue over relatively unimportant things? You don't really want to fight, and chances are, the other person doesn't either. So choose to be the bigger person and stop while you're ahead—and before somebody gets hurt.

Week 47

Father, teach me to be the kind of person who
loves peace. Show me how to be a peacemaker
in the middle of two valid but differing opinions.
Give me the power to walk away from an
argument before things get out of hand.

On Walking Away from a Fight

Today I will_____

_____

_____

_____

_____

_____

_____

_____

_____

_____

_____

The beginning of **STRIFE** is like letting out water, so quit **before** the quarrel breaks out.

PROVERBS 17:14

On Giving Up

Don't give up at the **FIRST** sign of
trouble; **hang** in there and fight.

PROVERBS 24:10, PARAPHRASED

I know things are tough, but you're tougher. You can get through this. The difficult circumstances you're facing right now are an opportunity for you to show God how much You trust Him. It's easy to have faith in God and say you believe He's good when things are rolling along relatively smoothly. It takes a whole other level of commitment to choose to trust Him when you can't see how He's going to come through this time. Say, "Lord, I believe. Help my unbelief." But don't give up!

Week 48

I am weak, God. I feel like a failure in so many areas of my life. I want to be a better mother. I want to stop yelling at my kids so much. I want to be more faithful in seeking You. Help me not to give up. You said that only a mustard seed of faith could move mountains. Well, that's about all I have. But I'm counting on that being enough because of Your promises to me.

Today I will_____

_____

_____

_____

_____

_____

_____

_____

_____

_____

_____

If you faint in the day of **ADVERSITY,** your strength **is** small.

PROVERBS 24:10

Wisdom in Action

201

Keeping It between the Two of You

If someone **HURTS** you, deal with the person **privately,** then forgive and *forget*. Don't discuss the incident with all of your **FRIENDS** first; otherwise, **everyone** feels the rift.

PROVERBS 17:9, PARAPHRASED

Wisdom for Today

When we feel hurt, the first thing we want is to be comforted. As little kids we ran to Mommy, who could always make it better. As moms we usually run to our friends. Most of the time that's a good thing. But in some cases we need to think twice before we pour out our anger and hurt to a friend, especially if another friend is the cause of our pain. If that's the case, we need to go directly to the offending friend and work things out. That way only one person—or at the most, two people—has some forgiving to do.

Week 49

Lord, You have forgiven me of so much; how dare I even consider not showing mercy to someone who has offended me? Help me to resist the temptation to air my grievances to other people. Let me be the kind of person who immediately comes first to You and then, with grace and mercy, directly to the person who has hurt me.

_____

_____

_____

_____

_____

_____

_____

_____

_____

_____

_____

Keeping It between the Two of You

Today I will_____

_____

_____

_____

_____

_____

_____

_____

_____

_____

_____

Whoever covers an **OFFENSE** seeks love,
but he who **repeats** a matter *separates*
close friends.

PROVERBS 17:9

On Being a People Pleaser

If you try to please **everybody** else, you'll tie **YOURSELF** up in knots. **Relax** and just concentrate on pleasing the **Lord**, and you will be fine. **HIS** is the only opinion that *matters* anyway.

PROVERBS 29:25, PARAPHRASED

As moms we can get so caught up in trying to please others that we end up failing everybody. Often we feel paralyzed, not knowing who to listen to. But we're never going to make everyone happy, so we might as well accept that and stop trying to, or we'll just be miserable. Our best bet is to find out God's opinion on the matter, act according to that, and let the chips fall where they may. If others have a problem with that, they can take it up with God. If the issue is one God doesn't specifically comment on in His Word, then ask the Holy Spirit for guidance. He will speak to you. I'm all for getting advice from other people, but ultimately, we need to be true to ourselves and the Lord. Be OK with that.

Heavenly Father, help me to care more about what You think than what anyone else in the world thinks. I want to be sensitive to other people's opinions and advice, but ultimately, You are the only one I have to answer to. Help me to obey You, even if I make somebody else mad in the process. Keep me free from being a people pleaser.

_____

_____

_____

_____

_____

_____

_____

_____

_____

_____

_____

_____

On Being a People Pleaser

Today I will_____

_____

_____

_____

_____

_____

_____

_____

_____

_____

_____

The fear of man lays a **SNARE,** but whoever **trusts** in the LORD is safe.

PROVERBS 29:25

On Interfering

Butt out and **DON'T** get into
the **middle** of an argument
that's *none* of your **BUSINESS.**
Otherwise, **they** may *turn* on you,
and **YOU'LL** end up **getting** hurt.

PROVERBS 26:17, PARAPHRASED

Why do we always think our opinion is so valuable? Are we really so proud that we think we can fix every problem? I know I have to guard against this presumption. Maybe it's a mom thing. After all, it's our job to have solutions and remedies at the ready. All I know is that I feel an almost irresistible urge to jump into every situation and try to fix it. It doesn't even matter if it's any of my concern. For some crazy reason, I feel as if I can solve all of life's little problems. What arrogance! Why would I set myself up to get caught in the middle, where nobody wins? I should just learn to keep my nose out of other people's business and give them some credit for being able to work things out on their own.

Week 51

Lord, help me not to interfere in areas where I have no place being. Remind me how foolish it is to invite even more trouble into my life by bringing someone else's problems into the picture. When I feel the need to help, quicken me to pray. After all, that's something I can do that will really make a difference!

_____

_____

_____

_____

_____

_____

_____

_____

_____

_____

_____

_____

_____

Today I will_____

_____

_____

_____

_____

_____

_____

_____

_____

_____

_____

Whoever MEDDLES in a quarrel not his own is **like** one who takes a passing *dog* by the EARS.

PROVERBS 26:17

On Being Beautiful

Good looks won't **LAST**, and flattery is just **lies.** Real *beauty* shines through a *woman* who loves the LORD.

PROVERBS 31:30, PARAPHRASED

Here's good news. It really is what's on the inside that counts! Ask any four-year-old boy, "Who's the most beautiful woman in the world?" His mommy! Ask any grown daughter caring for her aging mother the same question, and you'll get the same answer. Sure, beautiful features and a delightful personality are nice, but they're fleeting. With time even the most beautiful woman looks old, and the most sparkling individual gets cranky. The only truly stunning quality that will last is humility. And moms spend a lifetime humbling themselves in taking care of others. Nothing is more attractive. I wonder why we spend so much time looking in the mirror, investing in the temporary. Wouldn't it be smarter to keep our focus on the Lord, reflecting His heart of humility? Now there's real potential for beauty that is truly ageless.

Week 52

I want to be beautiful in your eyes, Lord. As I seek You with my whole heart, transform me into Your image so that I may reflect Your glory. When people look at me, I want them to see You and praise Your holy name. I adore you, Lord.

Today I will_____

_____

_____

_____

_____

_____

_____

_____

_____

_____

Charm is deceitful, and BEAUTY is vain, but a *woman* who **fears** the LORD is to be praised.

PROVERBS 31:30

Also available

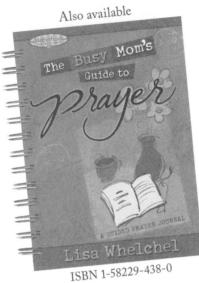

The Busy Mom's
Guide to
prayer

A GUIDED PRAYER JOURNAL

Lisa Whelchel

ISBN 1-58229-438-0

1 Busy Mom

10 Minutes a Day

20 Days a Month

120 Power-Filled Prayers

An Infinity of Blessing

HOWARD
PUBLISHING CO.

About the *Author*

Lisa Whelchel is best known for her role as Blair on the long-running television comedy *The Facts of Life*. Now a homeschooling mother, speaker, and pastor's wife, she is the best-selling author of *Creative Correction, The Facts of Life and Other Lessons My Father Taught Me*, and *So, You're Thinking about Homeschooling*, and *The Busy Mom's Guide to Prayer*. Lisa and her husband, Steve, are the cofounders of MomTime Ministries. They live in Texas with their children Tucker, Haven, and Clancy. For more information about Lisa, visit www.LisaWhelchel.com.